TEN GOOD RULES

BY SUSAN REMICK TOPEK
ILLUSTRATED BY ROSALYN SCHANZER

KAR-BEN COPIES, INC. ROCKVILLE, MD

*For Elayne, Carol, and the toddlers
who keep me writing.
For my parents and my girls with love.*
—SRT

Library of Congress Cataloging-in-Publication Data

Topek, Susan Remick.
    Ten good rules/Susan Remick Topek; illustrated by Rosalyn Schanzer.
        p.   cm.
    Summary: Intruduces the ten commandments from a Jewish perspective. Certain
commandments have been recast from negative to positive language for easier
comprehension.
    ISBN 0-929371-30-5. — ISBN 0-929371-28-3 (pbk.)
    1. Ten commandments—Juvenile literature. [1. Ten commandments.] I. Schanzer,
Rosalyn, ill. II. Title.
BV4656.T66   1991
296.3'85—dc20   91-32109
                                                                                        CIP
                                                                                         AC

Text copyright © 1991 by Susan Remick Topek
Illustrations copyright © 1991 by Roz Schanzer
Published by KAR BEN COPIES, INC., Rockville, MD 1-800-4-KARBEN
Printed in the United States of America.

Note: We have recast certain commandments from negative to positive language to
make them understandable to young children.

When the Jewish people left Egypt, Moses led them to a mountain in the desert. Moses climbed the mountain and talked to God. God gave Moses TEN GOOD RULES for the people to follow, so they could live happily together.

1

I am the
one and only
God.

2

Do not pray
to other gods.

3

Do not say
bad words.

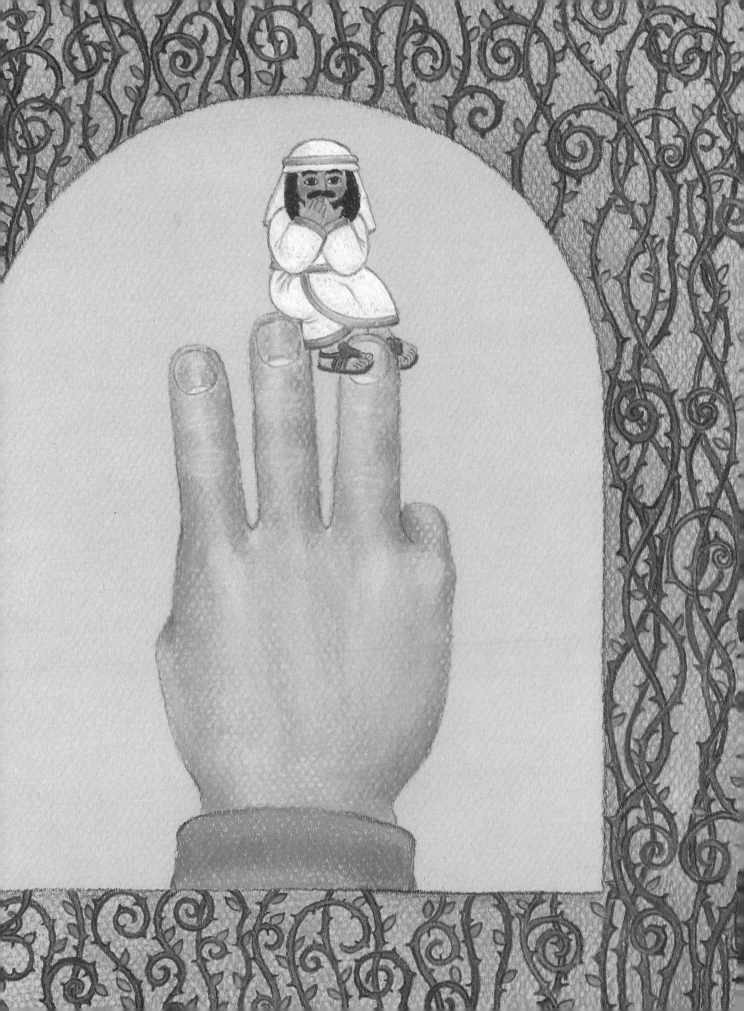

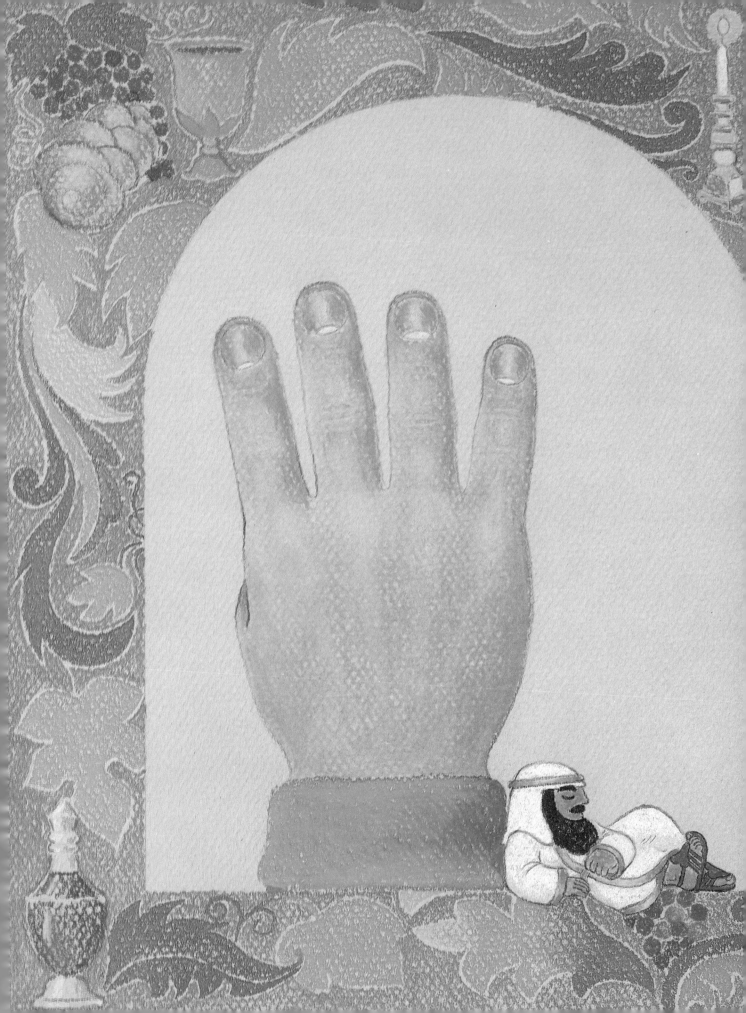

4

Celebrate
Shabbat.

5

Love your
father and mother.

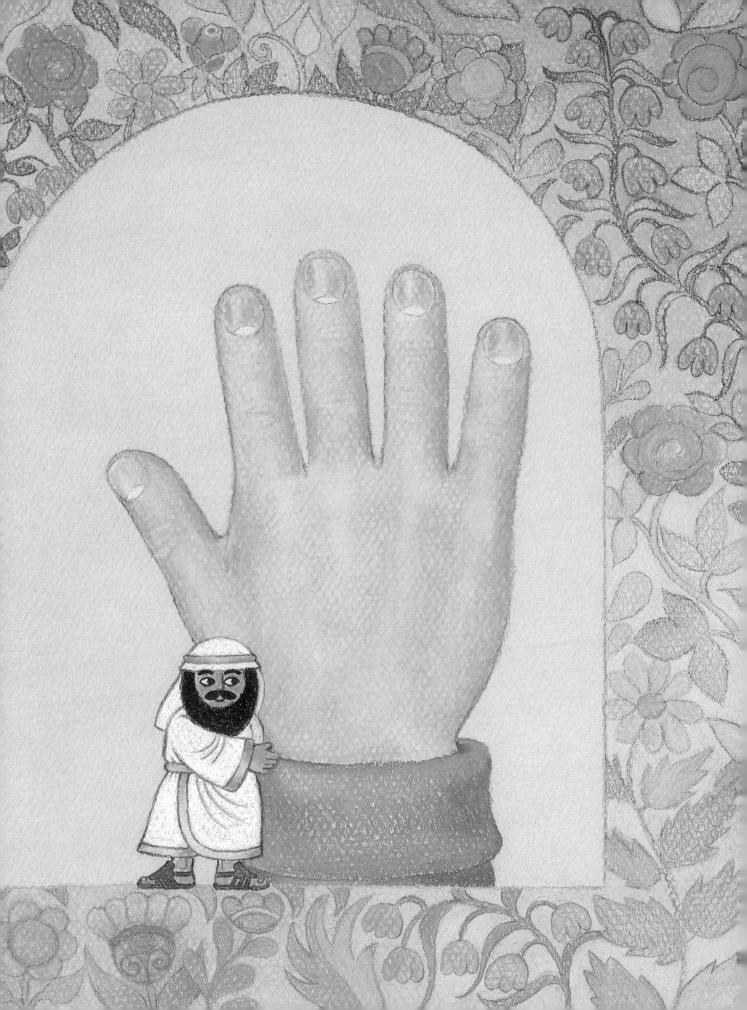

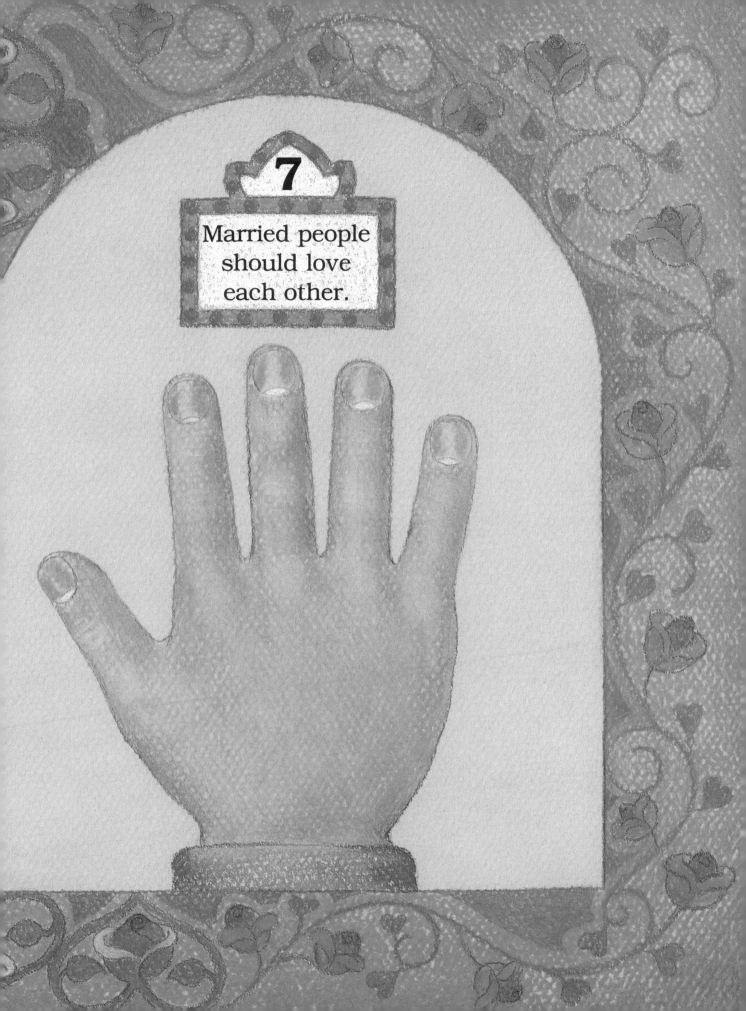

7

Married people
should love
each other.

8

Do not
take anything
without asking.

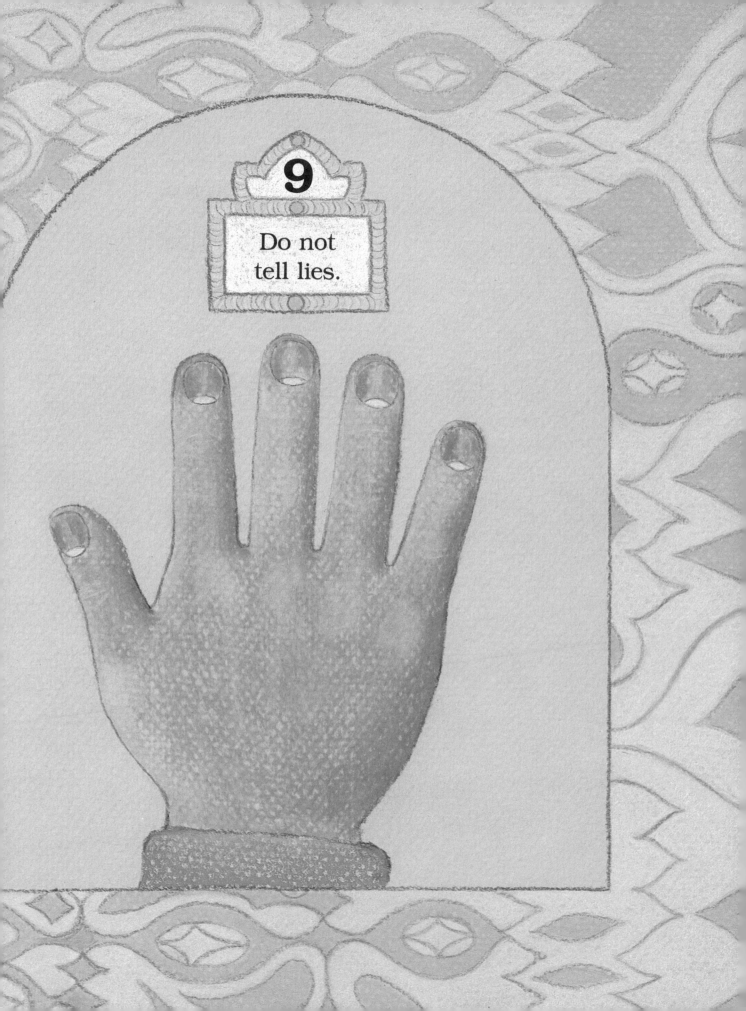

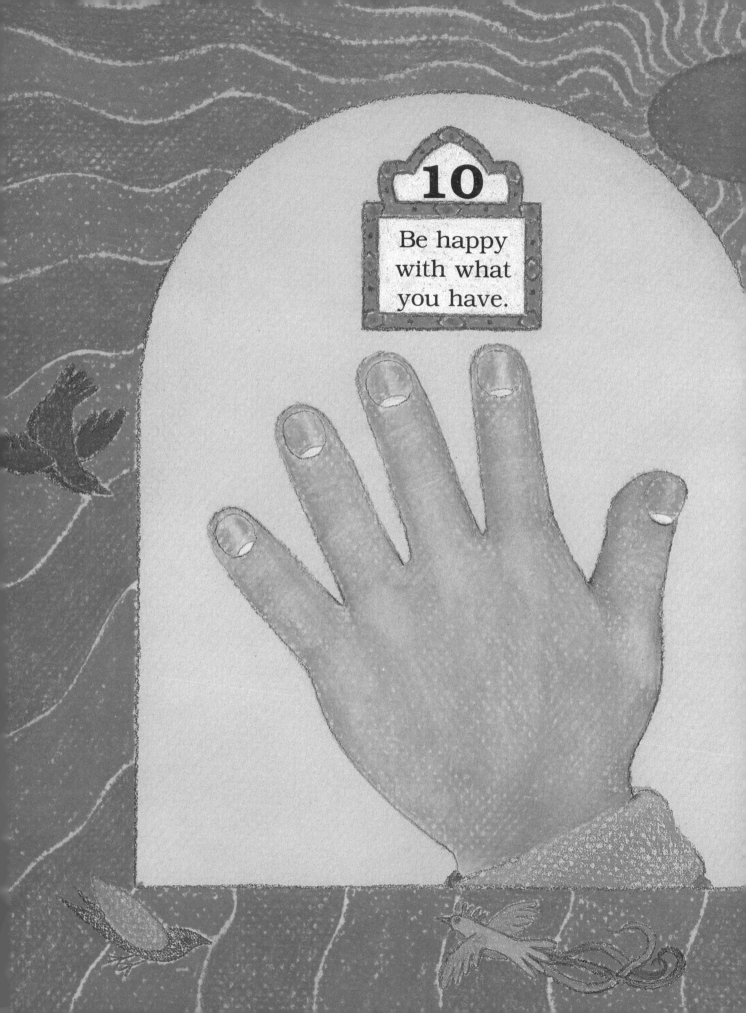

10

Be happy
with what
you have.

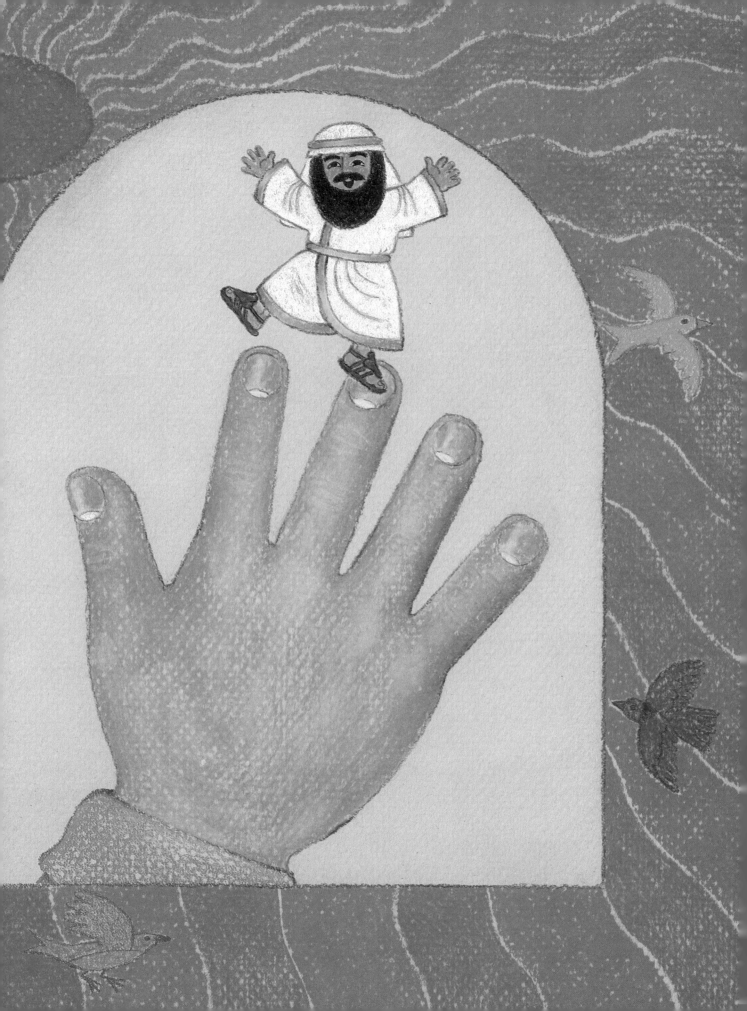

Moses told the people the
TEN GOOD RULES.

They listened and they
promised to follow them.
These TEN GOOD RULES
are just as important for us today.

About the Author

Susan Remick Topek holds a B.A. in Judaic Studies from the University of Texas, and has been involved in formal and informal Jewish education for more than 20 years. She lives in Setauket, NY with her husband and three daughters. She has also written *Israel Is* and *A Holiday for Noah,* both published by Kar-Ben.

About the Illustrator

Roz Schanzer is the illustrator of hundreds of books, magazines, posters, and filmstrips for children. She lives in Fairfax Station, VA, with her husband and two children. Roz has illustrated several books for Kar-Ben, including *Bible Heroes I Can Be* and *It Happened in Shushan.*